Linnaeus

K.W. Gullers–Birger Strandell

Linnaeus

Photo: K.W. Gullers–Peter Gullers–Björn Enström

Gullers International

Linnaeus

Carl Linnaeus – or Carl von Linné, as he called himself after receiving his title of nobility – is unquestionably one of Sweden's most famous scientists of all times, recognized primarily as a world-renowned botanist, one of the foremost who ever lived. He was by profession a doctor and a professor of medicine. Since, as a professor, he also dealt with botany, he was accustomed to identify himself as "Med. & Botan. prof. Upsal", which does not, however, tell the full story. He was a versatile person, who also occupied himself successfully with such other branches of the natural sciences as zoology, geology and mineralogy – and much more besides. In recent years he has been noted as an author of belles lettres and as a promoter of the art of printing in Sweden. His fresh, vigorous and, occasionally, rather coarse language is not to be found in the writings of earlier Swedish authors. In portions of his orations and descriptions of his travels, Linnaeus writes a prose that has the sound of the most beautiful poetry. Even today, Linnaeus exerts a strong influence on Swedish cultural life. He continues to attract the interest of doctors, natural scientists, historians, theologians and artists – to the great delight of the Swedish public. Overseas, interest in Linnaeus is also remarkably high. Indeed, nearly everyone is trying to discover some new aspect of the multifaceted Swede.

Linnaeus' first scientific work was written when he was still an eighteen-year-old "high school" student in Växjö. His years at the universities of Lund and Uppsala also resulted in some other promising works. He was, however, no more than a student to whom one could attribute high expectations, when, in 1732, he set out on his Lapland journey. When he returned, he was already an experienced scientist. His journey is regarded today as perhaps the most significant ever undertaken within Swedish borders. Linnaeus achieved his international breakthrough in the scientific world during his foreign journey (1735–1738) in the course of which he spent most of his time in Holland but also visited Germany, England and France. In Holland, where he established contacts with leaders in the nation's cultural life, the young Swede was cherished as never before. As the manager of "Hartekamp", the estate owned by the conspicuously well-to-do Georg Clifford, he had a free hand to pursue his own interests. Within the span of barely three years he now published 14 scientific treatises, including *Systema naturae*, which created a new era in the history of the natural sciences.

After his return from abroad, Linnaeus established himself as a physician in Stockholm for three years (1738–1741) during which he held public lectures in mineralogy and botany, was appointed physician of the Swedish admiralty and became one of the founders of the Royal Academy of Sciences. In 1741 he realized his dream ambition and was appointed professor of medicine at Uppsala University where, as noted, botany was also assigned to him. He assumed

The twinflower (Linnea) on the frontispiece, "My own flower" as Linnaeus himself called it. Photograph: Stig Ekström

his position at a fortunate time. While some work had of course already been carried out, botany was still in its infancy, lacking orderliness and the situation has been described, though somewhat exaggerated, as virtually chaotic. The entire planet was almost unexplored; a difficult and comprehensive job awaited execution. Collection and classification was the primary task, one for which Linnaeus was well suited. He had a capacity for sharp-eyed observation and immediately saw what no one else around him noticed. He also quickly perceived the significance of what he had seen and could then arrange his observations in accordance with his own classification methods. No laboratory was required for his pioneering work. This need did not arise until later, when the basic work had been carried out. This later research was perhaps delayed to some extent as a result of Linnaeus' dominant position.

The scientific climate at Uppsala was exceptionally stimulating. One publication after another flowed from Linnaeus' pen in a torrential stream and his reputation spread increasingly throughout the scientific world. In some quarters he met with opposition to his ideas; in others it was easier to win support. A team of eager and intellectually outstanding students – not only from Sweden but from all the corners of Europe – flocked around the master. There were even a couple from Africa and America. Linnaeus' lectures attracted great attention and reached an audience that extended far beyond the confines of his faculty. He could have two or three hundred persons attending his lectures while the other professors at the University had to be content with only a few, a situation which they naturally did not regard approvingly.

With the assistance of, primarily, the Swedish East Indian Company in Gothenburg, Linnaeus was able to send some of his best pupils to foreign countries throughout the world, travelling on Company ships, to make observations and collect information and materials, plants and other objects. Some pupils accompanied scientific experts on foreign expeditions. D. Solander was with James Cook on the latter's first voyage to the South Seas; A. Sparrman was on the second voyage. P. Forsskåhl was on a Danish expedition to the Arabian countries and P. Löfling conducted a Spanish expedition to South America.

As a result of Linnaeus' position as a researcher and academic teacher, Uppsala became the world center for the study of the natural sciences and during a thirty-year period little Sweden made a contribution in this field that is without parallel in the history of mankind.

Quite naturally, Linnaeus was even during his lifetime accorded many honours. He was made a nobleman (which was customary in those days) and was awarded the Order of the Polar Star (which was a great mark of distinction, never previously given to a scientist). He was made a member or an honorary member of many learned societies outside Sweden. The membership he prized most highly was that in the French Academy of Science, since he was the first Swede to be admitted and the number of foreign members was limited to eight.

With the years, the intensive work began to take its toll and Linnaeus occasionally felt exhausted, weak and depressed. Various ailments, pleurisy and the "Uppsala fever", were contributing factors. There were, however, no serious signs of illness until the early part of 1772 when he began to be troubled by dizziness and weakness in one leg; he grew thin and deteriorated. It may be suspected that he suffered from hypertension. In the spring of 1774 he was seized by a stroke, recovered slightly, but then grew increasingly worse. On January 10, 1778 he died in his home at Svartbäcksgatan in Uppsala, in his seventy-first year.

The home of the assistant vicar in Råshult, in the Swedish Province of Småland, marks the birthplace of Carl Linnaeus. He was born in "1707 at 1:00 a.m. on May 23rd, when spring was in beautiful bloom and the cuckoo had just announced the coming of summer."

The neighbourhood of his childhood home: "The vast number of stones and rocks makes the fields and pastures uneven and rough."

There Linnaeus found "the joys of my youth, the most delightful plants and flowers that grow wild in this place."

"In 1717, Carl entered the school in Växjö, where rude schoolmasters, with equally rude methods, instilled in the children an inclination to sciences that must have made the hairs on their heads stand on end."

Linnaeus' greatest interest was in the natural sciences. As an eighteen-year-old schoolboy, he wrote about poppy and its medical effects in his *Örtabok* (Book on Herbs) as follows: "Opium is made from its juice. Depending on how much one takes, this can bring on sleep for periods of one, two or three days, without awakening. Indeed, if one takes enough, one is not awakened before the sound of God's trumpet is heard."

In Lund, Doctor Kilian Stobaeus, later appointed Professor, took care of Linnaeus. Doctor Stobaeus "was a sickly man, blind in one eye, crippled in one foot and constantly tormented by migraines, hypochondriasis and backache; he was otherwise of incomparable genius."

Thus Linnaeus was afforded the opportunity to study thoroughly Sweden's southernmost province, Skåne, and thus was the first botanist to document and describe in detail its flora.

The Primrose (Primula veris L.) is one of the most beautiful spring flowers.

"Beech forests on both sides of the road; the great shade trees were tall and as if trimmed by Nature (so that a man could wander anywhere in the forest – moving freely under the branches – as in Virginian forests). The ground in the forest was covered with dry beech leaves."

A field covered with anemones (Anemone nemorosa L.) is also a welcome sight in spring.

Ox-eye daises (Chrysanthemum leucanthemun L.) in the meadow – Swedish summer.

The sight of a wren (Troglodytes troglodytes, L.) with its tail pertly awry was surely a source of inspiration for the student Carl Linnaeus, when he was out botanizing.

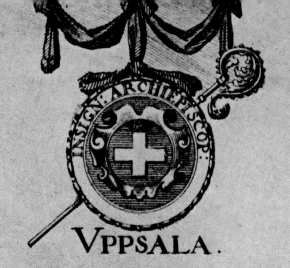

VPPSALA.

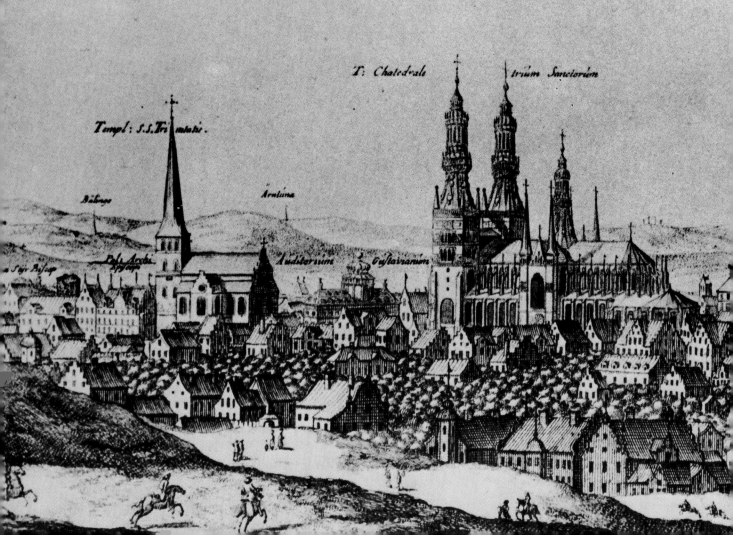

The view of Uppsala from the south when the almost penniless Carl Linnaeus on September 5th, 1728 made his unnoticed entry there as a student. A glimpse of the Gustavianum can be seen to the left of the cathedral spire. Gustavianum was built during the 1620s by King Gustaf II Adolf; its roof is crowned by Olof Rudbeck's Theatrum anatomicum, through which light enters from above in the same way as in the large old dwelling houses of the Vikings. Copperplate engraving by F. Akrelius in Busser's *UPSALA*.

"Rather unsettling that Linnaeus finds
Papillon to be of the fairer sex;
Cannot a man be beautiful in our minds?"
– The first three lines of Olof von Dalin's poem, "Betraktel-
ser Öfwer en Anmärkning om Fjärilar" (Reflections on an
Observation about Butterflies) – until now unnoticed in lit-
erature about Linnaeus.

King Carl's Sceptre (Sceptrum Carolinum Rudbeckii). In
1731, Linnaeus wrote his first thesis about this magnificent
Lapland Flower, which could be found during Linnaeus' time
and can still be found near Uppsala. However, it was
Rudbeck's son, Johan Olof, and not Linnaeus, who defended
this thesis. Linnaeus received an honorarium of 30 Swedish
riksdaler for his efforts; "that's why someone else had the
honour."

"Immediately after I was engaged by the Royal Society of Sciences on May 2nd to travel to Lapland and illustrate the countryside there in the *Three Kingdoms of Nature,* I gathered my things together and clad myself in the following garb: ... I left Uppsala on Friday, May 12th, 1732 at 11:00 a.m., barely half a day before my 25th birthday. Now the entire countryside, delightful, began smiling, now beautiful Flora is coming to sleep with Febus... Now winter rye was a quarter high and the barley was just showing its first leaf. The birch trees were ready to burst and leaves were appearing on all deciduous trees except the alder and aspen ...

We left Old Uppsala on our right with its three great hills – the ancestral burying grounds of the ancient Vikings...

Fluttering in the air above, larks entertained us with their song:
Ecce suum tirile, tirile, suum tirile tractat.

The sky was clear and warm, a westerly wind cooled and refreshed us with gentle puffs while the sky began to take on a dusky hue in the west."

The elk was not as common during Linnaeus' time as it is today, but could be seen occasionally in the forests of Norrland.

A beautiful, rippling stream impeded progress, but provided wonderfully fresh drinking water, highly appreciated by Linnaeus.

Ranunculus glacialis L. and Astragalus alpinus L. are two mountain plants, which, according to Linnaeus, can be found in Swedish Lapland and the Swiss Alps.

"Reindeer – like trees in the forest – were innumerable... About 2,000 came in the morning and were milked by men and women alike, standing on one knee." – Linnaeus later wrote a thesis on reindeer and one of his pupils, C.H. Hoffman, defended this thesis in 1754.

"Indeed I was now, for the first time, upon the Alps! Snowy mountains encompassed me on every side. I walked in snow, as if it had been the severest winter. All the rare plants that I had previously met with, and which had from time to time afforded me so much pleasure, were here as in miniature, and new ones in such profusion, that I was overcome with astonishment; thinking I had now found more than I should know what to do with... No roads, no trails, not a trace whatsoever of human life is seen... The green summer seems to have been driven out of this place and down into the deepest valleys between the mountains". July 6th 1732

2. Antecedenti quodam modo convenit *in* his omnibus, differt tn: *in* radice
   f. simulis antecedentium *omnes* plane *nigri*, *annus* autem *major*, *fere albi*;
   f. viride albis; *reliquis foliis*, *spicis* adeo *remotis* ut caulis *ruber* totus *ex arte*
   apparat. 3. quod *ramosior* sit, 4to quod non ita *cinerveset*.
   5. quod *fructifera* sit, petiolis *longioribus* bi-uncialis, *purpureis*, capitulis
   inter omnes maxima, globosis, oblique *prosilientibus*, viride
   calyptra *longe* minima, *pileacea*.

3. *vid est omnis* caule *et* foliis *sanguineis*; foliis *alternis* gradatim *majoribus*
   folia oblonga, *acuminata*, *spicas* ramuli capitulum *efformant*, *veluti* num. 5 *spicae*
   tota d *constructi*, *folia* inferiora capituli longior *interioribus*, *contra ac 1*.
   adeoq *majus est* 3. *spicae* *minor* 4. *quae e* petiolo *exit*; *purpurea*, *spicae*
4. *virescente* capitulo oblonga *piperiforma*, *dependentia est*.
   calyptra minor. *maj el foron in in eadem planta post*

5. Lichen *f. Marchsantia minima oblongifolia*, foliis *medio*
   angustatis *et* *facino asperis* *fuscis*

6. Culex *ibidem* maximus a me inventus est
   cujus figura vide omnis omnes reliquas Nis:

10. *Rubus fragaria folio, flore rubro.*
   radix *minima angusta filiformis*, *propagabilis*
   caulis *erecto* *rradice* radicem *figuranti*, *3½ 1. 4* *amplexicaulibus*, *fuscis vestit*
   lineisq noniss. *pubescit*, *semipedalis*, *flexilis*, *herbaceus*, *crassitie fili crassioris.*
   ut ex alis *singulis*, *longitudine ad caulis summum attingat.*
   Folia *alternatim fere, e caule egredientis, distincto spatio, ad alis 2 foliola ovata*
   3 lineas longas, 2 lata, obtusiuscula, crassiuscula, sessilia.
   petioli infra hoc *simplex, oppositi, supra salcati, infra convexi, semiunciales, ipsi*
   sustentant, e 2 laterulis sessilia, media petiolo propria in lineam longin infra.
   Folia *lateralia ovata* *sex, secundum nervum oblique, ita ut latus interius non b.*
   latitudine attingit exterius, margine inæqualiter profunde serrata
   folis aliis ovatis, glabris, plicatilis secundum varis q sulcis prominent.
   folis inferiis serpens omnis
   Flos faces caule l. ramis impositi, calyce univers conico, 5, 6, 7, laciniis ornatis, angustis,
   lanceolatis ovatis; latitudine lini. longitudin iis papal. virid.
   Pet. totidem quot laciniis, reflexus, falcato-ovata, plana, ungvis angustis ad calyciis minori
   calyce adnatis, purpureis altis
   flos innumeros ad unquis petali e calyce integro egredientis, brevissim, q interius serp in brevius
   super tota, in rosam pluripetal opicis d apparare ovat, purpureas, e spicis extin pilis albent
   dita laterula
   calyx pistillum complecenti, singuli q pistillo minimo instructa, ovaris q q ignoto oblongo albicant
   ornata, alternantim q hæc oia a spicis comitantibus.

Andromæda
ficta et vera.
Mystica et genuina.
figurata et depicta

Linnaeus' diary from his Lapland journey, *Iter Lapponicum*, 1732. The sketch at the bottom refers to this note: "Chamaedaphne of Buxbaum (Andromeda polifolia) was at this time in its highest beauty, decorating the marshy grounds in a most agreeable manner. The flowers are quite blood-red before they expand, but when full-grown the corolla is of a flesh colour. Scarcely any painter's art can so happily imitate the beauty of a fine female complexion; still less could any artificial colour upon the face itself bear a comparison with this lovely blossom. As I contemplated it I could not help thinking of Andromeda as described by the poets; and the more I meditated upon their descriptions, the more applicable they seemed to the little plant before me."

When Linnaeus first saw this plant "fixed on some little turfy hillock in the midst of the swamps, as Andromeda herself was chained to a rock in the sea, which bathed her feet, as the fresh water does the roots of the plant. Dragons and venomous serpents surrounded her, as toads and other reptiles frequent the abode of her vegetable prototype," he was reminded of the saga of Andromeda, the daughter of Cepheus, King of Ethiopia, and Cassiopeia, and named the flower in the marsh Andromeda polifolia.

Linnaeus' own pressed sample of Cyprideum calciolus L. – From the Linnean Society of London.

"The vast forests, although ruined in place, are of very little use to the general public. If it were possible to get these great logs, robust mast trees and solid timber for ships and building, down the (Dalälven) River to the sea without too much trouble and expense, the resources here would provide a timber supply for a long time." – Linnaeus in Särna, July 13th, 1734 during his Dalecarlian Journey. – This is the first recorded thought of log driving and of a Swedish forest industry. (following pages)

"The Falun Mine, Sweden's greatest wonder, is situated near the outskirts of the town.... A poet has never amply described Styx, Regnum Subterraneum and Plutonis or any other earthly hell as terrible as that seen here." – With this entry in his diary on August 17th, 1734, Linnaeus expressed his deep sympathy for the miners and their plight. (preceding pages)

In the beginning of 1735, Linnaeus became engaged to Sara Elisabeth Moraea, the eldest daughter of Johan Moraeus, a medical doctor in Falun. Shortly afterwards Linnaeus began his journey to Holland. Upon his return to Sweden, and when he had put his financial affairs in order, he "found harmony and joy in his work and applied for marriage. The wedding was held June 26th, (1739) at the Moraeus estate 'Sweden' near Falun, where Linnaeus finally won the hand of his beloved Sara."

Luscinia svecica L., a red-spotted bluethroat, with its resplendently blue 'bib' surrounding the rusty red star, is one of Sweden's most colourful birds. It is most common in the mountains of Lapland, but can also be found in the northernmost parts of Dalecarlia.

"In the beginning of 1735, Linnaeus travelled abroad with Claes Sohlberg, a medical student . . . He stayed eight days in Amsterdam to see as much of that city's splendour as he had time and money for. Linnaeus then travelled by boat to Harderwijk where he took examinations and defended a thesis and, finally, won his doctor's degree on June 24th." – In memory of him, a bust of Linnaeus now adorns the so-called Linnaeus Tower in Harderwijk, where all university studies were terminated many years ago.

Linnaeus stayed now " . . . with Clifford, with whom he lived like a prince; he had the largest garden for his studies, could order the plants and flowers not in the garden and buy the books that the library lacked. He was afforded every opportunity he could possibly desire in his botany studies. He also took full advantage of this and worked day and night." Beautiful illustrations of flowers were reproduced in the 18th century. This coloured engraving shows a lily, from *Uitgezochte Planten* by Christ. J. Trew.

Tab. XI.

LILIVM folus sparsis,   *multiflorum, floribus reflexis,*
fundo aureo, limbo auran-   *tio, punctis nigricantibus,*
pedunculis singulis   *unico folio instructis*

CAROLI LINNÆI, *SVECI,*

DOCTORIS MEDICINÆ,

SYSTEMA NATURÆ,

SIVE

REGNA TRIA NATURÆ

SYSTEMATICE PROPOSITA

PER

CLASSES, ORDINES,

GENERA, & SPECIES.

O JEHOVA! Quam ampla funt opera Tua !
Quam ea omnia fapienter fecifti !
Quam plena eft terra poffeffione tua !

Pfalm. civ. 24.

LUGDUNI BATAVORUM,
Apud THEODORUM HAAK, MDCCXXXV.

Ex Typographia
JOANNIS WILHELMI de GROOT.

The title page of Linnaeus' *Systema Naturae*, Leiden (Holland), 1735. This work consists of only 12 printed folio pages describing the three Kingdoms of Nature: animal, vegetable and mineral, with one page containing the key to the sexual system, i.e., a presentation of the 24 classes in the system. – The book immediately attracted the attention and interest of scientists throughout the world and formed the basis of a new epoch in the history of the natural sciences. The Grolier Club in New York lists the book among the 100 books considered to have made the greatest contributions to the development of mankind's knowledge of his environs.

In social life in Holland, Linnaeus was often the center of attraction. He often appeared in his Lapland dress, with Lapp trolldrum and all, as if to remind those around him of his pioneering efforts in researching a part of the world that was almost unexplored before his journey. It is not surprising that the Dutch were anxious to preserve this priceless sight in a portrait. Martin Hoffman received the assignment and painted three rather similar full-scale portraits of Linnaeus in 1737. This is a copy of the portrait which Linnaeus presented to his patron, J.F. Gronovius, as a token of his appreciation. It finally found a permanent home at the Linnaeus Museum in Uppsala just a few years ago.

"Stockholm received Linnaeus as a stranger in September, 1738. Linnaeus intended to live there, working as a physician, but as he was unknown to most and few dared place their cherished lives in the hands of an 'untested' doctor." – It was difficult at the beginning for Linnaeus, who opened a practice in the Old Town in the hope of receiving patients from the Skeppsbron district (Stockholm harbour). Eventually, he had his breakthrough, however, built up the biggest medical practice in the city and was successful in other fields, too.

The Tessin Palace in Slottsbacken (Castle Hill) in Stockholm, where Linnaeus moved from his simple dwellings in Österlånggatan. Here he was taken care of by the powerful Carl Gustaf Tessin, who offered him "free lodgings, in the chambers he once occupied himself as a bachelor and free meals." – This is not the most common view of the Tessin Palace; it shows the backyard as it was during Linnaeus' time and still is up to this very day.

The House of the Nobility in Stockholm (Riddarhuset). "In the year 1739 A.D. at 09:00 a.m. on June 2nd. For the first time, Messrs. Ahlström, Andr. Höpken, S.C. Bielke, Carl Linnaeus and Mårten Triewald met in the Auditorio illustri to discuss the establishment of a proposed society." – In this beautiful building, surely Stockholm's finest, the Royal Swedish Academy of Sciences was founded with this statement from the minutes of the Academy's first meeting.

"Before adjourning, (Swedish) Parliament (1761) resolved that those raised to the nobility by His Majesty be made permanent peers, retroactive from April 4th, 1757." – Linnaeus' own rather clumsily written draft of his coat of arms.

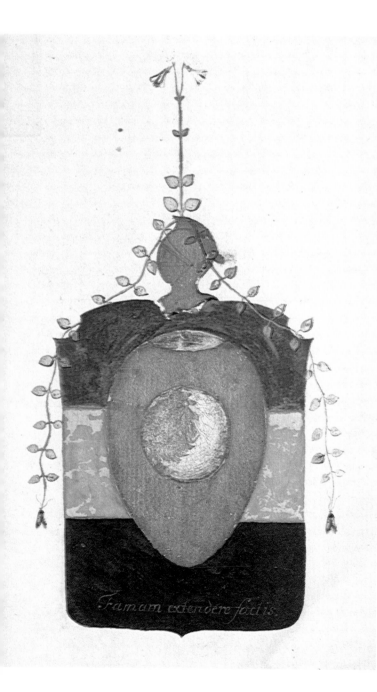

"Consider how amorous dragonflies mate and tell me if Venus assigned similar marriage laws to any other species. The male flies about, here and there through the air, with his forked tail, like a pair of tongs. When he sees his mate, he snatches hold of her with his tail around her neck so she is taken with him by force, as a hen taken by a hawk. She may try to escape his grasp by curving her tail into a hook beneath her to the male's breast (exactly to the point where Venus has hidden Cupid's arrows) and is thus won as if by violence without violence."

"As soon as we touched the shore of Öland we realized that this was a land which was altogether different from the rest of Swedish provinces.... There were many windmills on the *lantborg*, especially on the western side."

Holcus lanatus L., the beautiful grass Linnaeus found on the islands of Öland and Gotland as well as on his two other official journeys.
Photograph: Stig Ekström

"Blåkulla is a little island, situated between the northern point of Öland and Småland, which old hags and fairy tales dedicate to Pluto, and not to Neptune.... If any place in the world looks dreadful, this is it.... We left Blåkulla in the late afternoon, wind and waves propelled our boat; Blåkulla lay between the sun and our little ship." – June 15th, 1741.

Visby, Gotland. "The town seemed to us like a model of Rome. ... It was not very large, on the land side confined within a high wall, in which were many substantial and old towers; the wall is surrounded by two dilapidated embankments." – June 23rd, 1741.

A bumble-bee (Trichius fasciatus) in a beautiful flower (Campanula glomerata, L.)

"This Hoburg is one of the most remarkable things that Nature has made on all Gotland; it is very high, like a most beautiful castle." – July 9th, 1741.

Gotland abounds in orchids. Jungfru Marie Nycklar (Dactylorchis maculata L.)

"Stora Karlsö, the larger of the two small islands off Gotland, was very high, except for the south cape, with a horizontal infertile level on top, similar to the *alvar*-land on Öland." July 14th, 1741.

This rare plant, Lactuca quercina L., was found by Linnaeus on his brief visit of only a few hours to Lilla Karlsö, the smaller of the two islands, on July 14th, 1741. "I had never before had the opportunity to see this plant, and Ray is the only one who has described it so clearly that one can be sure that he has such a plant." – Despite intensive efforts by several botanists, the plant was not found in Sweden again until nearly 200 years after Linnaeus' initial discovery, the second time on the larger island, Stora Karlsö. – Photograph: Stig Ekström.

"The razorbills flew rapidly around the boat several times without fear, and although we shot at the birds, they did not go away but became even more eager to fly above our heads." – July 14th, 1741. – Neither do our present-day guillemot on Stora Karlsö seem afraid of humans. Here they are obviously curious of the photographer and what he is up to.

Fritillaria meliagris L. (Kungsängsliljan) was discovered at Kungsängen, south of Uppsala, by Linnaeus' friend, Sten Carl Bielke, sometime in the early 1740s, Linnaeus wrote in his *Flora Svecica*, 1745.

"The old stone house, built by Olof Rudbeck the elder, stripped of wood but with iron pillars and beams, looked like an owl's nest; it was renovated later and used as the Professor's residence." Linnaeus and his family lived in this house from 1743 to 1778.

Linnaeus' lecture room on the second floor, where he gave private lessons.

Linnaeus' charter of nobility and coat of arms, as it appeared after clearance by the national heraldist. "However, (Daniel) Tilas, the armorist censor, changed it completely."

"In 1743, the orangery and its two wings were finished and the garden was put in repair with many foreign plants, which each year grew in number as Linnaeus received new seeds from friends and business associates abroad." (preceding pages)

"Gothenburg, a city somewhat smaller than Uppsala, was the loveliest of all Swedish cities." – Linnaeus on his Västgöta Journey, July 9th, 1746. – View of Gothenburg from Skansen Götha Lejon, coloured copperplate engraving, by J.F. Martin.

"The manufacturing industry was established here in Alingsås, where everything and everybody seemed to revolve around the industry. ... There are no beggars here; when they do come, they are immediately put into the factories."

Nevertheless, the Swedish artist Carl Larsson succeeded in 1882 in getting a picture of Linnaeus astride a horse with a beggar in front of him – before the man was recruited by the industry. – Linnaeus on his Västgöta Journey, July 6th, 1746.

"The fortress in Marstrand is called Carlsten; situated high on a sharply sloping mountain of rock, a landmark for mariners. – Prisoners, sentenced to Marstrand to pay for their imprudence and rash acts, found themselves in misery, and would certify that the walls were invincible. Anyone who has seen these poor souls wouldn't wonder that the hairs on the head of the listener will often stand on end when he hears the name of Marstrand mentioned." – July 15th, 1746.

"Nature's gifts here in Sweden's west coast waters are so numerous, so rare and unknown, at least to those in Sweden who are living far away from this ocean, that we were taken aback by it.... We botanized on the ocean floor as if in a second Sweden." – July 16th, 1741. – Photograph: Tomas Lundälv.

"The rocky islets between Kyfkil and Marstrand looked, in fact, like the landmass on the other side of Kyfkil when it had been under water, so that only the tips of the rocks broke the surface of the water; these islets consisted mainly of small, rounded and rocky hills, naked islets and several sunken rocks and one can expect that after a thousand years this archipelago will have the same appearance as the land-mass above has today." – July 15th, 1746.

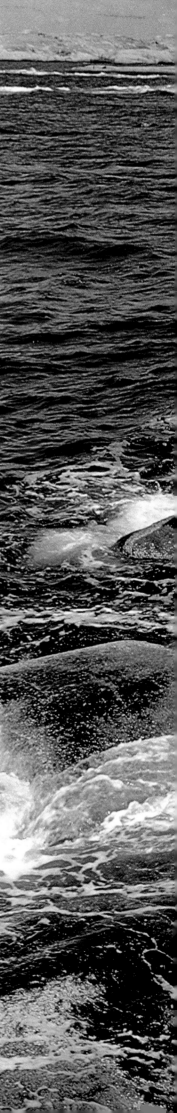

"Storks seldom dare fly north of Skåne; they are seen daily strutting on their long legs across the plain and building their large nests in trees and on roofs near the villages." – Linnaeus on his Skåne Journey (3), according to Sixten Belfrage.

"The plain that extends towards Lund, Malmö and Trelleborg begins here in Dalby; it conjures up an image of Canaan with its glorious pastures and beautiful grain fields as far as the eye can see."

"There is unquestionably no other part of Sweden quite like Skåne."

1762. "Linnaeus built a dwelling-house at Hammarby; as he began to feel tired and wanted to provide for his children and their future." Linnaeus' Hammarby is situated 10 kilometers south of Uppsala. He spent the summers there with his family and often celebrated Christmas there, too. Students bearing banners flocked to Linnaeus' Hammarby to attend a lecture or to accompany him on botanical field trips (preceding pages).

There is a small museum in the western wing of Hammarby; it contains a large collection of Linnaeus' pictures, mostly copperplates and lithographs and a few busts.

The interior of 'the Museum' with fish-skin in the ceiling, bookshelves, a herbarium cupboard, Linnaeus' lectern-chair, "study horse" and the seats where his pupils sat during lectures. The lectern-chair and seats are still used by the Swedish Linnaeus Society at annual spring meetings, usually held outdoors in front of 'the Museum'.

"1769. In his drawing room at the estate the walls were decorated with drawings of herbs from the East and West Indies, and in his bedroom of hand-painted plants, rather dear and very beautiful. Surely no other wallpaper is more splendid or more expensive."

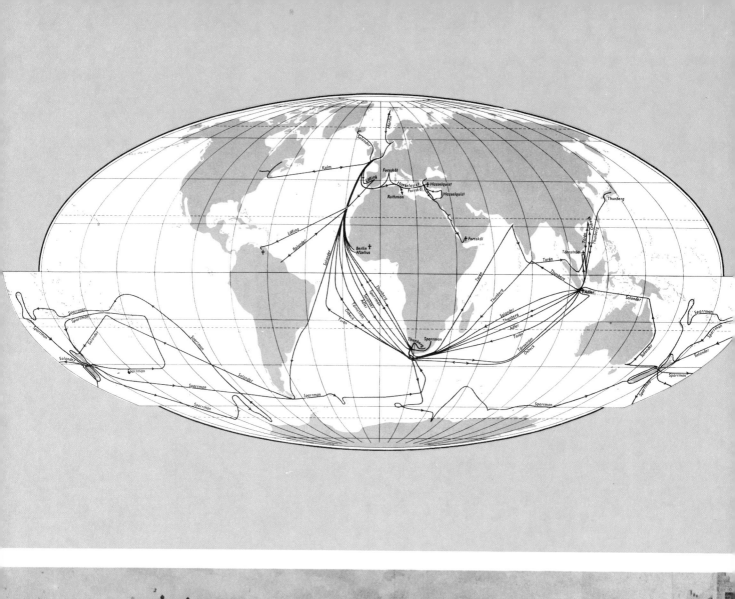

This is not a map of an airline's or shipping company's traffic routes, but rather an illustration of the far-reaching research trips made throughout the world by Linnaeus' pupils. These journeys were made possible by the inspiration provided by Linnaeus in Uppsala and the generous cooperation of several enterprises, especially the Swedish East Indian Company.
The chart was drawn up in 1950 by Professor Rob. E. Fries.

Arabic war exercises in Yemen, an adventure experienced by P. Forsskåhl, a pupil of Linnaeus.

"1747. For many years Linnaeus had spoken in support of a journey to North America for his pupil, Pehr Kalm. Linnaeus also assisted Kalm in obtaining scholarships and a professorship in economics at Åbo. When this was accomplished, Kalm was indeed dispatched to America."

The mountain Laurel, the state flower of Pennsylvania in the U.S., was given the name 'Kalmia' by Linnaeus in honour of his pupil, Pehr Kalm. – Photograph taken at the Point State Park in Pittsburgh, Pennsylvania.

LINNÉ

welcome
learned neighbor
e university of chicag

The Linnaeus Statue in Lincoln Park, Chicago, Illinois, was officially unveiled May 20th, 1891. The statue was moved in 1976 and dedicated again at the new site in front of the University of Chicago by His Majesty, Carl XVI Gustaf, King of Sweden, during his visit to the U.S. during its bicentennial year. This replica of the original statue, by F. Kjellberg, in Stockholm's Humlegården Park, was sculptured by K.J. Dyfverman after Kjellberg's death.

During his America journey, Pehr Kalm visited Niagara Falls. He described the famous falls in a letter to his friend, Benjamin Franklin. Excerpts of Kalm's letter to Franklin were published in the latter's newspaper, the *Pennsylvania Gazette*, September 20th, 1749. This was the first description of the falls in English on record, surprisingly written by a pupil of Carl Linnaeus.

"1746. When the charter with the East Indian Company was to be renewed, Count Tessin, Councillor of the Realm, included a clause whereby the shipping company was obliged to provide one free passage annually to China for a student of natural history." – As a result of this agreement, Linnaeus was able to send his pupils all over the world as ship's doctors and chaplains on the company's boats. When Linnaeus visited Gothenburg during the summer of 1746, construction of the East Indian Company's magnificent building in Norra Hamngatan, Gothenburg, had not yet begun. The building was completed in 1760.

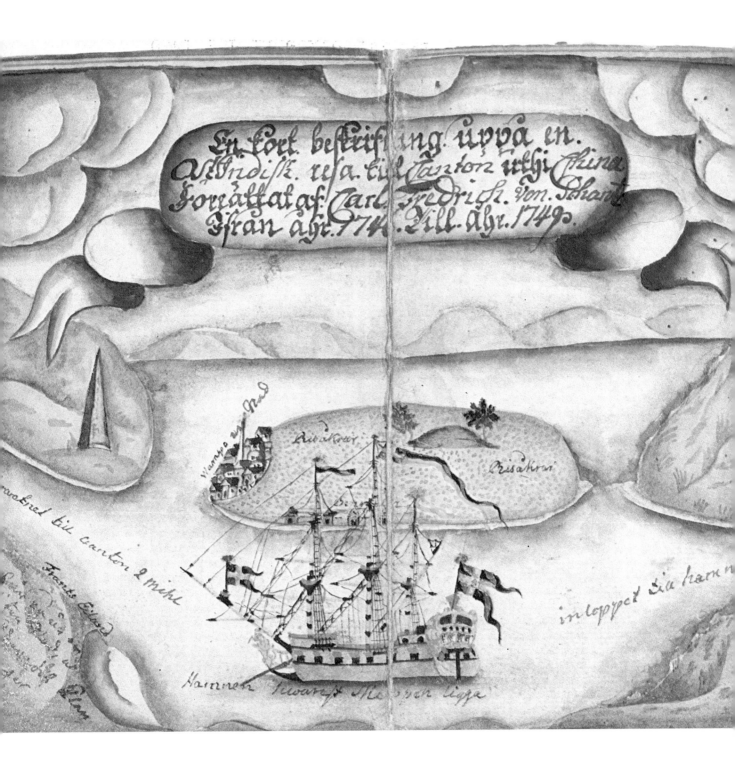

The title page of "A brief narration of an East Indian journey to Canton in China,... 1746 – 1749," by Carl Fredrich von Schantz. – Manuscript with an East Indian traveller at the anchorage in Wampoa. – From the Royal Library, Stockholm.

CAROLI PETRI THVNBERG

MED. DOCT. PROF. REG. ET EXTRAORD. ACADEM.

CAES. N. C. REG. SCIENT. HOLMENS. SOCIET. LITTER.

VPSAL. PATRIOT. HOLMENS. BEROLIN. N. SCRVT.

LVNDIN. HARLEMENS. AMSTELDAM. NIDRO-

SIENS. MEMBRI

FLORA IAPONICA

SISTENS

PLANTAS

INSVLARVM IAPONICARVM

SECVNDVM

SYSTEMA SEXVALE EMENDATVM

REDACTAS

AD

XX CLASSES, ORDINES, GENERA

ET SPECIES

CVM

DIFFERENTIIS SPECIFICIS, SYNONYMIS PAVCIS,
DESCRIPTIONIBVS CONCINNIS ET
XXXIX ICONIBVS ADIECTIS.

———————————

LIPSIAE

IN BIBLIOPOLIO I. G. MVLLERIANO

1 7 8 4.

Journeys by Linnaeus' pupils resulted in a great many
travel books, published in several editions in various foreign
languages, as well as many other scientific treatises. One of
the most important of these, *Flora Japonica*, was written by
Carl Peter Thunberg. It was the first scientific work on the
flora of Japan and led to the reference to Thunberg as "the
Linnaeus of Japan." Through his travel books and other
manuscripts, Japan was introduced in its proper light for the
first time in the Western World. Even today, Thunberg
serves as an invaluable link between the sciences of Japan
and Sweden.

E KAEMPFER

C P THUNBERG

This monument in Nagasaki honours the memory of E. Kaemfer and C.P. Thunberg, the latter of whom was in Nagasaki during most of his Japanese visit in 1775–76. As recently as the spring of 1976, Thunberg's memory was honoured again in Japan at a Swedish-Japanese symposium at the University of Tokyo.

Linnaeus shows the details of a plant to listeners in the great outdoors. – Lithograph from the 19th century.

Daniel Solander, another pupil of Linnaeus, settled in London and was a member of James Cook's first expedition to the South Seas. – Medal minted in 1911 by Erik Lindberg for the Royal Swedish Academy of Sciences.

Carl Peter Thunberg, who made the Japan Journey, succeeded the master as Professor at the University of Uppsala (1784). – Medal by Erik Lindberg, 1906.

"Mr. Inlander has made such a masterful wax model of me; everyone says they've never seen anything quite so masterful and with such likeness." – Medallion in plaster by C.Fr. Inlander, 1773.

The memory of Linnaeus and – as is fitting – many of his pupils have been honoured in several different countries through the issuance of postage stamps in conjunction with jubileums and anniversaries, in many cases with pictures of the men being honoured. Postage stamps series are also often issued – with illustrations of plants and animals, followed by the Latin name and its creator. In Linnaeus' case, the capital "L" is sufficient.

(next page)

Linnaeus

His passing was proclaimed by the King of Sweden, speaking from the throne, an honour never accorded any other Swede before or since until Dag Hammarskjöld, the Secretary General of the United Nations, was honoured in the same way nearly 200 years later, following his tragic death in Africa. At regular intervals, at home and abroad, Linnaeus' memory has been honored in a manner that goes far beyond the tributes paid any other Swede. The dates of his birth and death are those principally celebrated, as well as those marking the publication of his most important works, such as *Systema naturae* (1735) and *Species plantarum* (Species of plants, 1753), and of his travel books. During the present century we have been able to follow Linnaeus' life virtually from cradle to grave in the perspective of 200 years. The contributions of his disciples have also received their due share of acclaim, abroad as well as in Sweden.

No Swede's image has been reproduced as diligently as Linnaeus'. He sat as a model for only a few artists: the Dutch Martin Hoffman, and Sweden's own well-known portraitists, J H Sheffel, Gustaf Lundberg, C F Inlander, Per Krafft the elder, and A Roslin – and perhaps a few more. Hundreds of other pictures have been produced, based on the originals created by these artists. Statues or busts of Linnaeus have been set up in many botanical gardens or public places throughout the world. Hundreds of medals have been struck in his honour, most of them outside Sweden. In recent decades Linnaeus' memory and – as is fitting – that of his disciples have been honoured through the issuance of postage stamps, largely in countries other than Sweden. Linnaeus has given his name to streets, squares, bridges, ships, schools and gardens. Even entire cities abroad have been named after him. He is commemorated in the names of sports clubs and art galleries and many learned societies and scientific organizations, the most active of which is the Linnean Society of London, located in Burlington House in the heart of the world metropolis. There, most of Linnaeus' herbarium, library and surviving manuscripts are preserved in a worthy manner.

Linnaeus was extremely productive. His published works can be counted in the hundreds. Many of them were issued in new editions and were then generally edited and expanded to include new findings. The twelfth edition of *Systema naturae*, issued during 1766–1768, the last to be edited personally by Linnaeus, consists of somewhat more than 2,500 octavo-size pages and differs most significantly from the first edition of 12 printed folio pages. Nearly all of the pupils' 186 dissertations which list Linnaeus as the praeses were written by him. Linnaeus also found time to write letters. Several thousand have been preserved. He corresponded with more than 70 foreign scientists, writing in

Linnaeus assumes a more free and easy pose for a statuette amid lilacs in a private garden than when he stands erect as in the officially dedicated statues in Chicago and Stockholm.

Latin since he had never learned a living foreign language. Nearly 900 of his letters in Swedish are in the library of the Royal Swedish Academy of Sciences. Linnaeus also wrote a number of treatises that were not published until long after his death. Some still remain to be published.

Against this background it is easy to understand that the literature dealing with Linnaeus has reached enormous proportions. Very few persons have become the object of such attention. The books and scientific articles can be counted in the thousands and the newspaper articles total close to 10,000. No other scientist has been written about so extensively.

Interest in Linnaeus has fluctuated over the years, but never seems to wane. However he may be regarded, his unique contribution cannot be denied. The "sexual system" in botany was of major significance when it was presented by Linnaeus. It survived him for many years, later to give way to a more natural system – a development that Linnaeus himself had already anticipated. What remains is his great importance as a classifier and breaker of new ground. The nomenclature of both plants and animals continues to be based on works written by Linnaeus: the first edition of his *Species plantarum* (Stockholm, 1753), and the first volume of the tenth edition of his *Systema naturae* (Stockholm, 1758). In both works, Linnaeus had introduced the so-called binary system of nomenclature; he had given each species a name consisting of two words, a generic name and a specific name, which represented a major simplification and precision in terminology. This brilliant concept alone, coupled with the enormous work required to carry it out, would have been adequate to assure Linnaeus one of the more prominent niches in the history of the natural sciences. But he did so much more. He created an era!

His unique life story is merely one example in human history of the fact that a genius creates his own success only through his own strength, even if – like Linnaeus – he comes from "a root without trunk".

Linnaeus died January 10th, 1778 at home in Svartbäcksgatan in Uppsala. He was buried in the Uppsala Cathedral January 22nd. He lies at rest together with his wife and son, Carl, just to the right of the main entrance. In 1798 friends and former pupils erected a monument made of Älvdal porphyry decorated with one of Sergel's bronze medallions. Now placed in a chapel near the grave, the monument is often visited by school children, who listen as their teachers tell them briefly about Carl Linnaeus, surely one of the most remarkable scientists Sweden – and the world – has even known.

CAROLO a LINNÉ
BOTANICORUM
PRINCIPI
AMICI ET DISCIPULI
MDCCXCVIII

"The generosity of the Chevalier Roslin is unique. He has promised to take off my head at no cost. (Linnaeus' own description of having his portrait painted.) His normal fee for a portrait is between 7,000 and 8,000 dalers." The result "was splendid – nothing can be more exact; the likeness in all the others is lacking compared with Roslin's." – A copy of the Roslin portrait, 1775, by Oscar Björk.

The Uppsala Cathedral at dusk. A picture of the exterior in modern times.

Copyright: © K W GULLERS 1977
Photography: KW Gullers, Peter Gullers, Björn Enström,
Östen Matsson, NATURFOTOGRAFERNA
Text: Birger Strandell
Design: Jan Bohman
Printing: Usines Brepols, Belgium
Publisher: Gullers International Inc, Chicago U.S.A.
ISBN 91-85228-42-7